T5-DHS-075

Dear SanTa Paws

Letters to Santa from Dogs

Dear SanTa Paws

Letters to Santa from Dogs

Compiled by E.J. Sullivan

SWEETWATER
PRESS

SWEETWATER
PRESS

Dear Santa Paws: Letters to Santa from Dogs

ISBN-13: 978-1-58173-717-2
ISBN-10: 1-58173-717-3

Book design by Miles G. Parsons
Illustrated by Neal Cross

For Sadie and Waldo

Dear Santa Paws,

Is there sumthing you could bring to chew on that would last a littel longer? That wuld be grate.

Your friend,
Bizz

Dear Santa,

I wish for my own remote kontrol for the TV. When everyone leeves in the morning then I could watch whatever I want.

Gus

Dear Santa Paws,

    I hope you don't miss our house this year because it is a little hard to see—down by the raleroad trax just a little shak like maybee some boxes stuk together it isn't much but me an my frend Bill we are verry happy and we hav each other. Thank you Santa!

Mike

Dear Santa Paws,

   If you culd bring a blanket to keep my puppies warm it would be the best Christmas ever.

                                            Sunshine

Dear Santa,

Don't take this the rong way but there are too many cats around here. Could you bring us a cat door so I could chase them outside once in a while?

Thanks,
Cowboy

Dear Santa Paws,

I wish I didn't hide those bones out in the yard so good, I don remember wher they all are now. Santa, if you wuld bring me one more reel big bone I promise I wont hide it or burie it and it will the very best present I ever got. You are the best!

(I am being a good dog.)
Soupy

Deer Santa Paws,

    We hope we are on yer gud dogg list. But pleeese Santa, we don't know exackly what it takes to get on the list. We try reel hard not to chew (on the rong things), chase the kats, bark at the UPS man, jump up on people, get on the furrnichure, eet the garbage, or eet the kat's food. But this is a verry long list of things NOT to doo. Culd you please tell us what are some other things we CAN do to get on yer good doggie list.

                    Thanx and wee luv you!
                    Huck and Belle

Dear Santa Paws,

I wuld like a can openr verry much plees. You are a dog's best frend!

Sinceerly,

Bear

Dear Santa,

I know ther are not enuf homes to go around but if you culd just find a place for me to stay for Christmas it wuld be ok, I wuldn't have to stay forever. But I wuld like to stay forever in sum ones home, especly if it had childrun.

Tony

Dear Santa,

I wuld like a dog friend. Cud you bring my peeple a puppy for Christmas? Make it smaller than me and not too loud.

Thank U!
Happy

Dear Santa,

I don't get around like I used to. Once, I could outrun even the mail truck, jump over fences, and leap up onto my boy's bed in a single bound. Christmas is coming and I sure do want to be around to share it with my boy. That's all I want, Santa, just to be there when my boy comes down the stairs with those eyes of his shining at what's under the tree.   Sincerely,
                    Old Mackie Boy

Dear Santa,

Where do you live? Are you up in heaven with Jesus and the angels? Is that how you make miracles happen? If that is right I want to thank you Santa for letting me get adopted by these nice people. I am not hungry any more and they play with me. You don't have to give me anything else, Santa. Take care of another doggie as many of my friends need homes too.

Your loving friend,
Mitzie

Dear Santa Paws,

Is there something that it is ok to shred to little peeces that nobody will care about? If so I wuld like a verry big bunch of those. Anything will doo. You are the gratest!

Love, Pigpen

Dear Santa,

We hav a kat & she sez I am stoopid. Will you pleez tell her shee is rong?

Xoxoxox
Buford

Dear Santa Paws,

My boy used to play ball with me and we went for long walks and stuff, and even went swimming. Then I ran with him on his bycicle and we went for sum trips in the car too. But now my boy isn't here verry much, Santa, and I am verry sad. Can you bring me back my boy, please?

Sincerely,
Rufus

Deer Santa,

There is something under the house that smells reel bad, it is driving me krazy I want to get at it SOOO much! Kuld you get it out for mee?

                    Bud

Dear Santa,

If you can make reindeer fly, can you make dogs fly too?

Sissy

Dear Santa,

There is this dog across the street I really like that is soooo kute and I really like him. He is a lot smaller than me but that is ok, I still love him. Santa, can you do sumthing to make him notise me?

Love always,
Muddy Girl

Dear Santa,

The other dogs make fun of me bekause I am kind of funni looking. I don't remember my mom or dad but one must have had a big head and one had short legs. I am really kute and lovving inside and I sure wish some nice familie would come thru here and get me out of this kage to where I could start being their dog.

Your frend,
Sammy

Dear Santa Paws,

I need a whole bunch of tennis balls, kwik before anybodie notices what happened to the old ones.

Your pal,
Butch

Dear Santa Darling,

I desperately need a new coiffure. My owner insists on taking me to the less expensive styling salon and they simply do not have any clue how to do my fur. I like more of a bouffant on top with a pom pom on the end of the tail. And please – pale pink only on the toenails? Please, please dear Santa Paws get me to a new groomer!

Kindest regards,
Boopsie

Dear Santa Paws,

Iz it possibl to ask for some kat food? I don't know if that wuld be rong or not. If it is, just forget this letter and bring me some dog food – the canned kind. (But I reely like cat food the besst!)

Yer friend,
Diego

Deer Santa Paws.

Pleeze bring us some dog biskits, the kind that come in the orange box and taste like chickin. We are leeving out for you some kat food (ha ha)…it is the best thing ever. (You culd bring some of that too but make sure the owners giv it to us & not the kats)

Love,
Patsy and Terry

Dear Santa,

I wish my people wud take me to the park. I am home alone all day when they go to werk and then they cum back and go out again. I shure wud like to run around outside and em lonesome.

Sidecar

Dear Santa,

I wuld like to no, do you hav a dog? If not I wuld like to be yur dog. Let me no asap.

Yore futchure dog,
George

Dear Santa,

I wud like to ask for a friend to play with. When my people go to work I am al alone al day long. There is a bird heer in a kage but it is not verry smart. I wont repeet what it sez to mee when our people aren't here. Anyway so if you have a little dog or puppie that wud like a home with a gud friend to play with wud you please bring it to our house on Christmas?

Sincereest regards,
Hoagie

Dear Santa Paws,

Wee liv in a bigg bilding and ther are lotts of other dogs in it I know becuz I heer them barking sumtimes but I nevr see them or play with them becuz my people are relly bizzy and do not hav a lott of time too take me outside too play. Santa, cud you bring my people more time?

Your true blue frend,
Razzy

Deer Santa Paws,

Our cat just had kittens. I cant beleeve this but we are going to need a bunch more doggs around here now. Can you please help me to have some puppies? Thank you deer Santa.

Your faithful
Skippy Sue

Deer Santa,

I promise to lern some manners if you will jus not let them send me back to that obedeeance skool. I will do anything you say. Pleeze help!

Yer frend,
Max

Dear Santa Paws,

We hav hung up our stockkings and shure would like it more then annything if you cud please fill them with some garbage—sevveral dayz old is ok!

Sinceerly,

Puggs and Muggs

Deer Santa Paws,

There iz one thing I want more than anything else on earth and that is a skwirrel. I hav been trying to katch one for about 3 years now. So maybe you better just bring me one. Anny size skwirrel is gud.

Keep up the gud werk!
Truman

Dear Santa Paws,

I wissh you could bring my owner some kind of new job so she wont have to travell so much and leave me allone so much. I tore out the part of the newspapper that sez Help Wanted but I don't think she notised and she scolded me and threw the papper away. Well it did make a littel more of a mess then I planned. But I only wantted her to be with mee more. Culd you pleese bring her a new job?

Roxie

Dear Santa Paws,

I promise I wil never chase another kar if yoo will please bring me a chew bone, a ball, or a frisbee.

Dylan

Dear Santa,

I am so sorry for what I did, I did not mean to be a bad dog. It is just that when I am alone I get so nervous and next thing you know I am chewing. I know that was our best chair and I am not supposed to be near it. I will never ever EVER do it again, I promise Santa!

Yours,
Bingle

Deer Santa,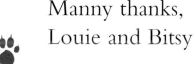
    Pleese bring:
- Bones – any kind
- Canned food (dogg or kat)
- Annything that squeakz
- A sofa we can stay on and not get in trubble
- Those treats that come in the foil pouchs
- Leftoverrs
- A bigger yard w/ a place to digg holeses
- Cheez!!!!!

Manny thanks,
Louie and Bitsy

Hi Santa Paws,

You don't no me but I saw you at the shelter putting up the Giving Tree and I just want too put in a word for sumeone to hanng a star on the tree for me.

Your friend,
Shadow

Dear Santa Paws,

The kats r making me rite this which iz not fair. They hav my favritt stuffd toy, it iz a munkey, an wont giv it bak until I write sumthing. I do not think they ken reed so it is ok, this will bee just between U and Me. Santa, culd U please doo sumthing about these Kats?!!!! (They think I em askin U for real tuna fish.)

Seriusly,
Ben

Dear Santa,

Iz it tru that you see everything? Then you kno how much I like shoez. Slipperz are pretty grate too. I want too be a gud dog, an I am thinking that if I had my own shoez to chew on it wud be ok. So if you ken bring sum that wud be good. Oh, and my boy wud reelly reelly like a bicicle.

Dodger

Dear Santa Paws,

I am simply dying for a manicure. The bichon across the street has her nails AND hair done every week! All I ask is just one time to look that great, pluss I am a poodle so I desserve it – rite? Thank you darling Santa.

> Luv and kisses,
> Lulu

Deer Santa Paws,

I no I em not supposed to like kats but there is this one next door that I think mite be a little sweet on mee. Shee keeps getting up on the fense and waving her tale and then purring and gets down and brushed all around my leggs. It is a little embarrassing, I like her but I don't think this is appropriat. Can you please tell her I am a dog or send her a nother kittie to have a krush on?

Manny thanx,
Chester

Deer Santa Paws,

Ken you show mee how to open the refrigerator?

Biskit

Dear Santa Paws,

My owner went to heaven. Can you tell me how to get there?

Sincerely,
Marty

Dear Santa,

I have lost my favorite bone, culd you help mee find it?

Chuck

Dear Santa,

My owner is blind so I am writing this for her. She would really like to have sum new dresses. You see everything so you know her size and everything. It wuld be a reely nice surprise for her. Thanx a million, Santa!

Love,
Sheba

Deer Santa Pawz,

　　Wher do kats come frum? Cud you please make them go back ther, wherever it is? That wud be the best Chrismass present you cud giv to all us dogs. Thank you!

Yer frend,
Jax

Dear Santa,

I am so lonely here at the dog pound. There are a lot of other dogs around but I miss my family. I didn't mean to run away, I just got lost. Could you please tell my family to come and get me????

Poppy

Dere Santa Paus,

I work as a watchdog and I shure wuld like some kind of entertanement to keep me awake during these long nite hours! Kuld you send a kute gurl dog, a portable tv, or a eye-podd? Yur help is appreeshiated!

Yer frend,
Duke

Dear Santa,

   A big old bone, a patch of shade, and a lazy afternoon are about all this dog could ask for. Merry Christmas.

                              Blue